Kevin McCollum   Roy Miller   Boyett O
Stephanie McClelland   Barbara Freita

present

Music and Lyrics by
Lisa Lambert and Greg Morrison

Book by
Bob Martin and Don McKellar

by Special Arrangement with Paul Mack

Starring

Danny Burstein   Georgia Engel   Sutton Foster   Edward Hibbert   Troy Britton Johnson
Eddie Korbich   Garth Kravits   Jason Kravits   Beth Leavel
Kecia Lewis-Evans   Bob Martin   Jennifer Smith   Lenny Wolpe

and

Andrea Chamberlain   Jay Douglas   Stacia Fernandez   Linda Griffin
Angela Pupello   Kilty Reidy   Joey Sorge   Patrick Wetzel

Scenic Design
David Gallo

Costume Design
Gregg Barnes

Lighting Design
Ken Billington
Brian Monahan

Sound Design
Acme Sound Partners

Casting by
Bernard Telsey Casting

Hair Design by
Josh Marquette

Makeup Design by
Justen M. Brosnan

Orchestrations by
Larry Blank

Dance and Incidental
Music Arrangements by
Glen Kelly

Music Direction and Vocal
Arrangements by
Phil Reno

Music Coordinator
John Miller

Production Supervisors
Brian Lynch
Chris Kluth

Production Stage Manager
Karen Moore

Associate Producers
Sonny Everett
Mariano Tolentino, Jr.

Press Representative
Boneau/Bryan-Brown

Marketing
**TMG - The
Marketing Group**

General Management
**The Charlotte
Wilcox Company**

Directed and Choreographed by
Casey Nicholaw

American Premiere produced at the Ahmanson Theatre by Center Theatre Group, LA's Theatre Company

Cover art courtesy of SpotCo

ISBN 978-1-4234-2565-6

7777 W. BLUEMOUND RD. P.O. BOX 13819 MILWAUKEE, WI 53213

In Australia contact:
Hal Leonard Australia Pty. Ltd.
4 Lentara Court
Cheltenham, Victoria, 3192 Australia
Email: ausadmin@halleonard.com

For all works contained herein:
Unauthorized copying, arranging, adapting, recording or public performance is an infringement of copyright.
Infringers are liable under the law.

Visit Hal Leonard Online at
www.halleonard.com

The Drowsy Chaperone marks the beginning of Lisa and Greg's writing collaboration.

Photo by Bob Martin

Prior to *Drowsy*, Lisa was best known for writing and performing songs with Toronto comedy troupe Skippy's Rangers (Jonathan Crombie, Lisa, Bob Martin, Paul O'Sullivan and Scott White), and for creating the Toronto mini-hit *Honest Ed: The Bargain Musical* (co-written by Brock Simpson, John Mitchell and Steven Morel).

Greg's background includes touring with The Second City, scoring and musically directing shows for Canadian horror clowns Mump & Smoot (Mike Kennard and John Turner), and years of musical collaboration with Toronto writer/performer Karen Hines and director Sandra Balcovske.

Since *Drowsy*, Lisa and Greg have written songs for stage and TV, most notably the television series "Slings and Arrows."

Greg and Lisa would like to acknowledge fellow *Drowsy* authors Bob Martin and Don McKellar, director/choreographer Casey Nicholaw, and musical wizards Glen Kelly, Phil Reno and Larry Blank for their contributions to the score. And a big thanks to the creative team in Toronto, especially Janet Van De Graaff whose name enhanced many a lyric, and Matt Watts, who insisted a monkey be in the show.

The Drowsy Chaperone

CONTENTS

6   Cold Feets

13   Show Off

22   As We Stumble Along

29   I Am Aldolpho

33   Accident Waiting to Happen

38   Toledo Surprise

48   Bride's Lament

59   Love Is Always Lovely in the End

63   I Do, I Do in the Sky

69   I Remember Love

COLD FEETS

Words and Music by LISA LAMBERT
and GREG MORRISON

Copyright © 1999 Lisa Lambert and Gmorr Inc.
All Rights Reserved   Used by Permission

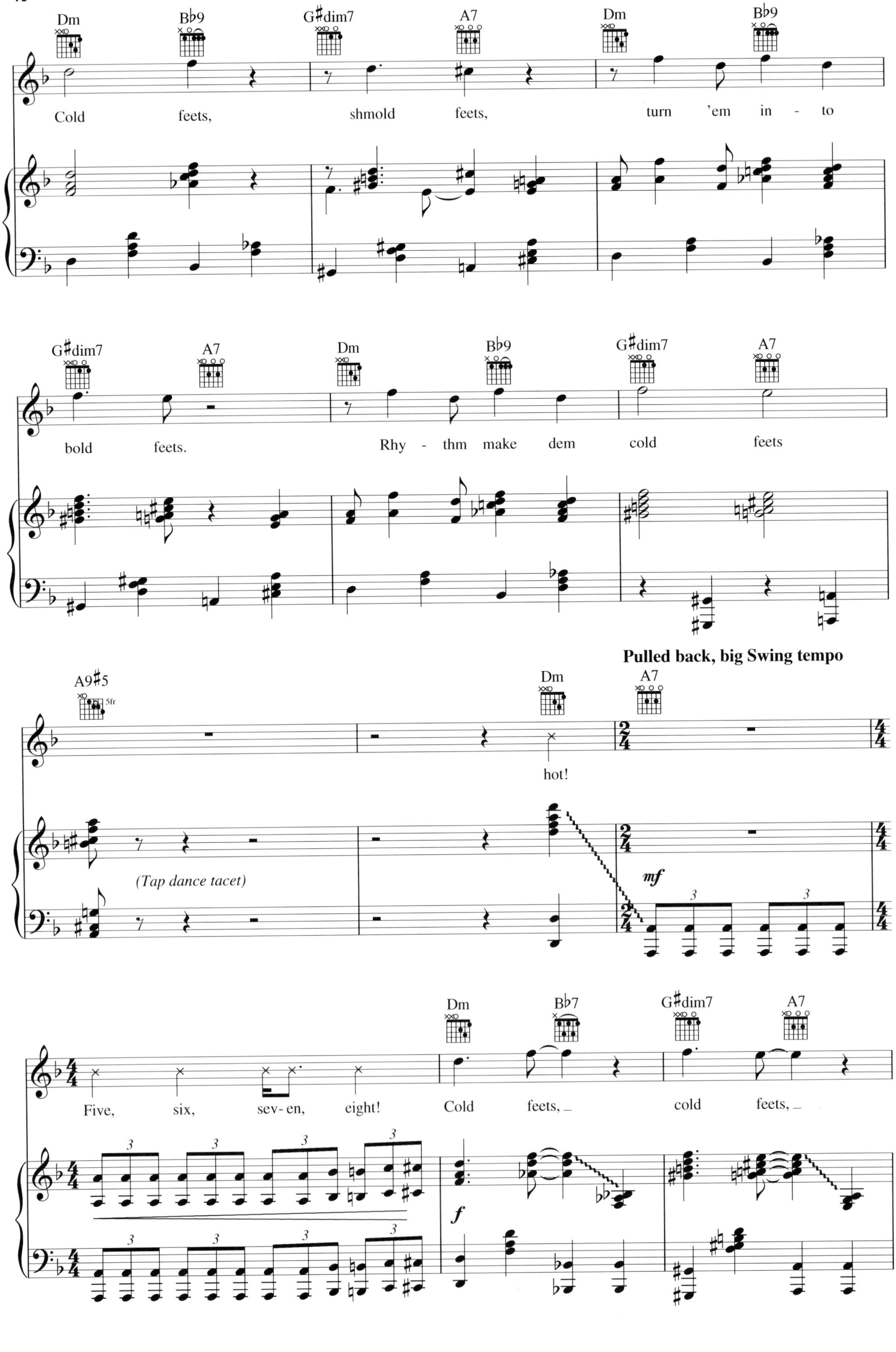
Dm
B♭9
G♯dim7
A7
Dm
B♭9
Cold feets, shmold feets, turn 'em in - to
G♯dim7
A7
Dm
B♭9
G♯dim7
A7
bold feets. Rhy - thm make dem cold feets
Pulled back, big Swing tempo
A9♯5
5fr
Dm
A7
hot!
(Tap dance tacet)
mf
Dm
B♭7
G♯dim7
A7
Five, six, sev- en, eight! Cold feets, cold feets,
f

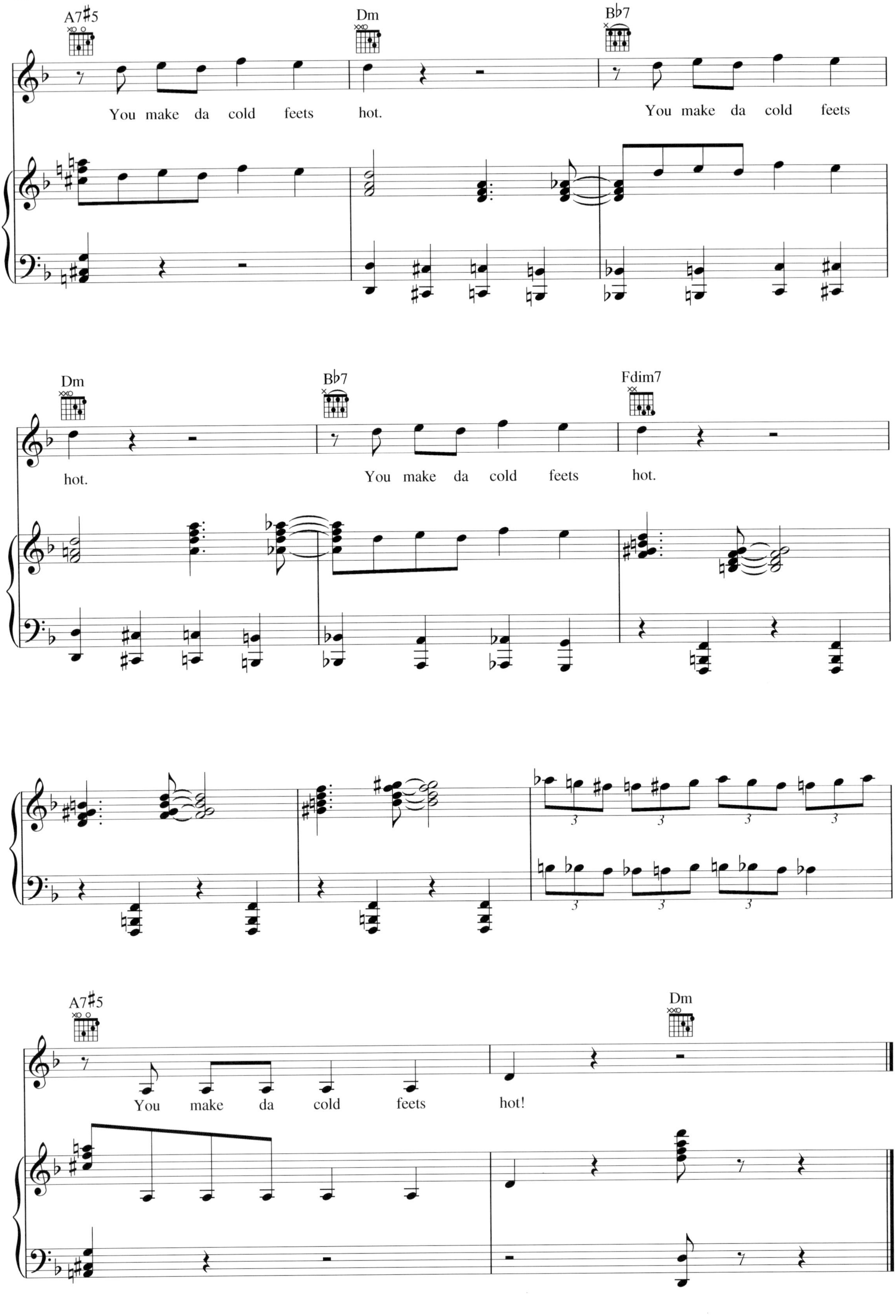
A7♯5
Dm
B♭7
You make da cold feets hot.
You make da cold feets
Dm
B♭7
Fdim7
hot.
You make da cold feets hot.
A7♯5
Dm
You make da cold feets hot!

SHOW OFF

Words and Music by LISA LAMBERT
and GREG MORRISON

Copyright © 1999 Lisa Lambert and Gmorr Inc.
All Rights Reserved   Used by Permission

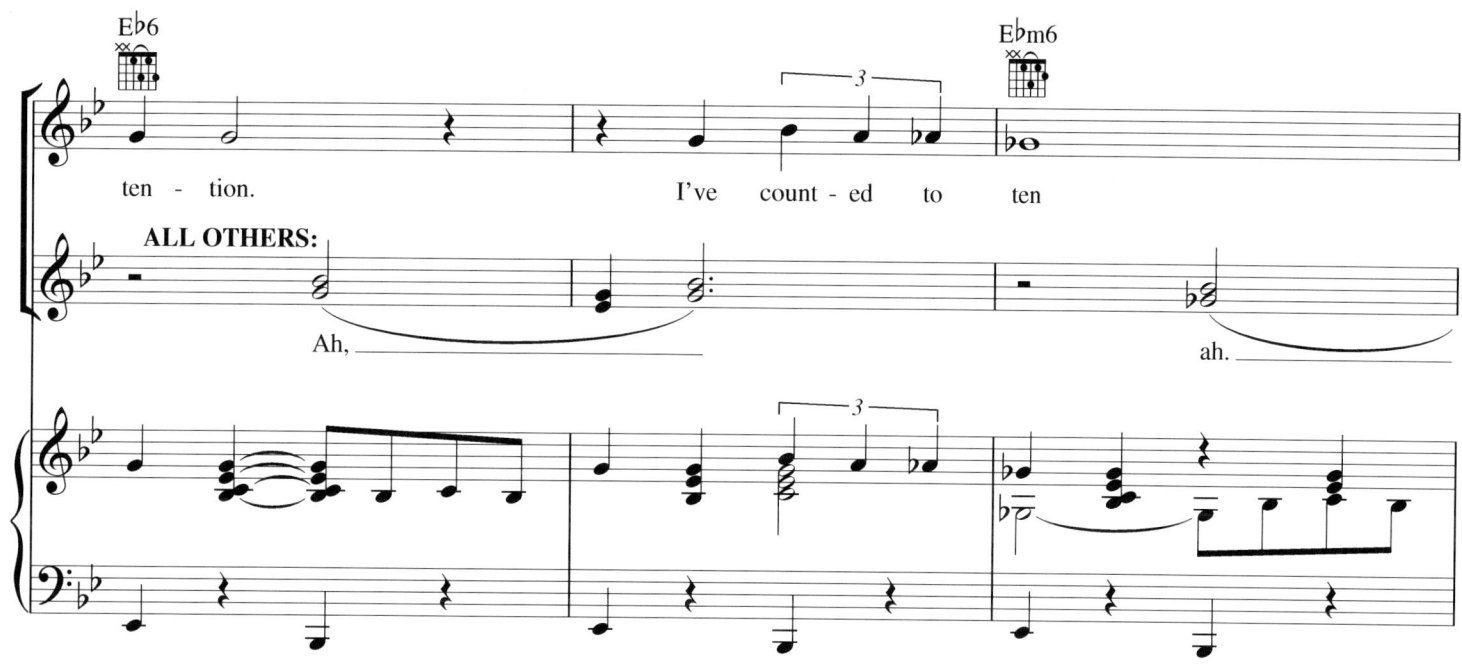

AS WE STUMBLE ALONG

Words and Music by LISA LAMBERT
and GREG MORRISON

DROWSY: As we stumble a-long

on life's funny jour-ney,

as we stumble a-long into the blue,

Copyright © 1999 Lisa Lambert and Gmorr Inc.
All Rights Reserved Used by Permission

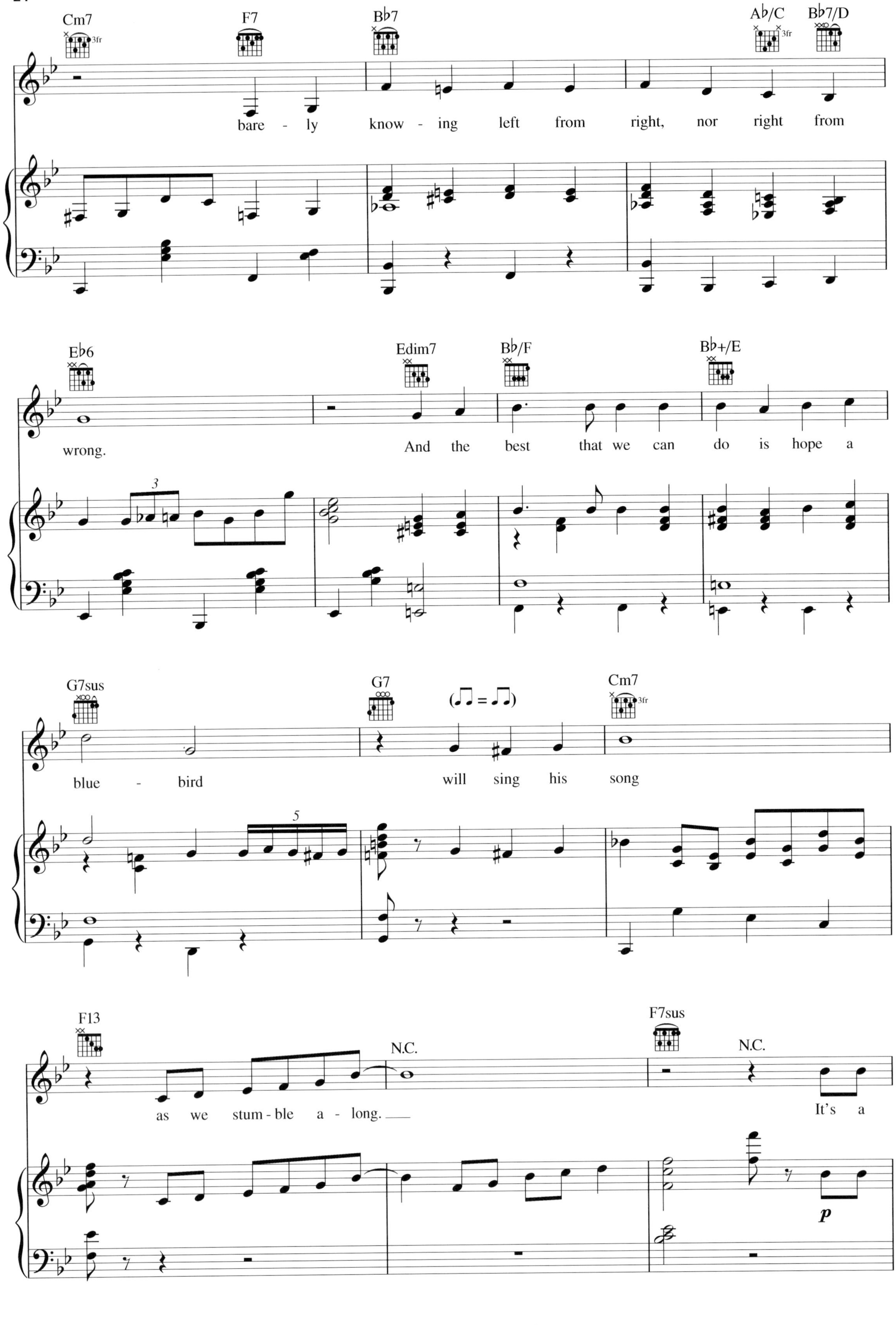
Cm7
F7
B♭7
A♭/C
B♭7/D
bare - ly know - ing left from right, nor right from
E♭6
Edim7
B♭/F
B♭+/E
wrong. And the best that we can do is hope a
G7sus
G7
Cm7
blue - bird will sing his song
F13
N.C.
F7sus
N.C.
as we stum - ble a - long.
It's a
p

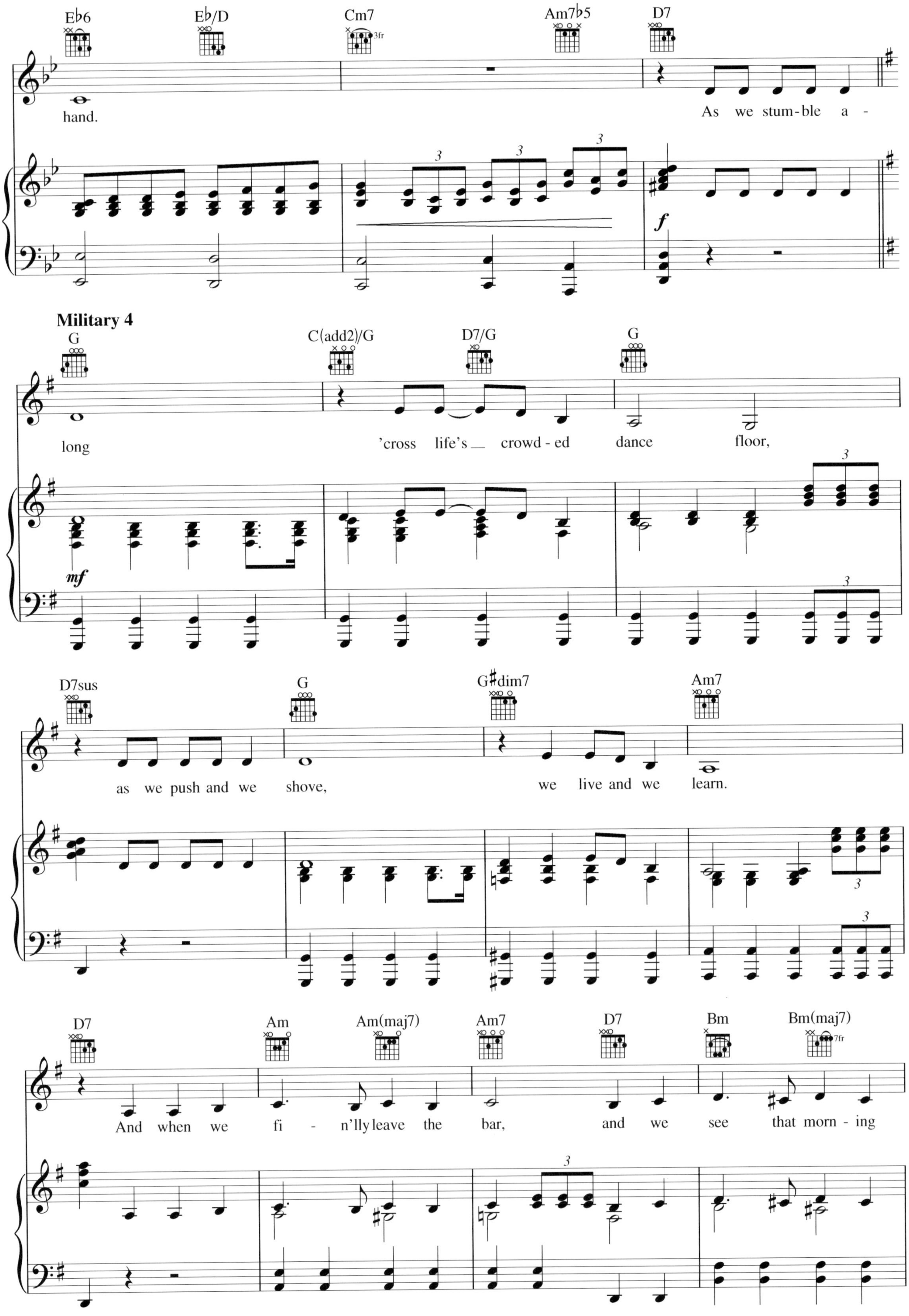
Eb6
Eb/D
Cm7
3fr
Am7b5
D7
hand.
As we stum-ble a -
f
Military 4
G
C(add2)/G
D7/G
G
long
'cross life's crowd-ed
dance
floor,
mf
D7sus
G
G#dim7
Am7
as we push and we
shove,
we live and we
learn.
D7
Am
Am(maj7)
Am7
D7
Bm
Bm(maj7)
7fr
And when we
fi - n'lly leave the
bar,
and we
see that morn - ing

I AM ALDOLPHO

Words and Music by LISA LAMBERT
and GREG MORRISON

ACCIDENT WAITING TO HAPPEN

Words and Music by LISA LAMBERT
and GREG MORRISON

TOLEDO SURPRISE

Words and Music by LISA LAMBERT
and GREG MORRISON

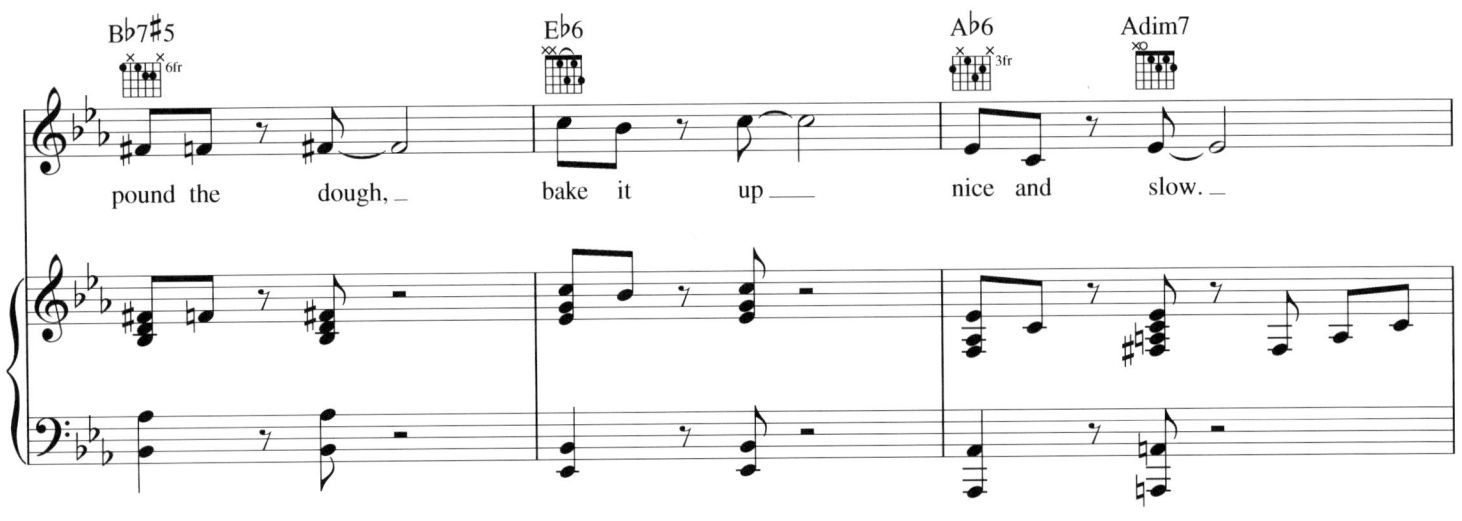

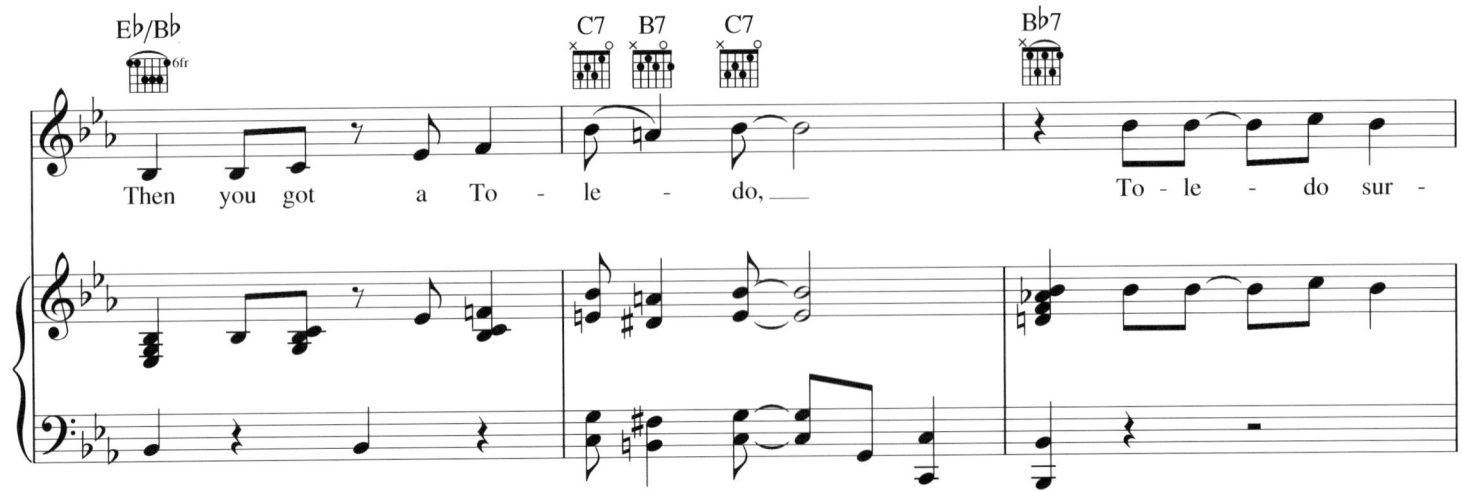

Copyright © 1999 Lisa Lambert and Gmorr Inc.
All Rights Reserved   Used by Permission

44

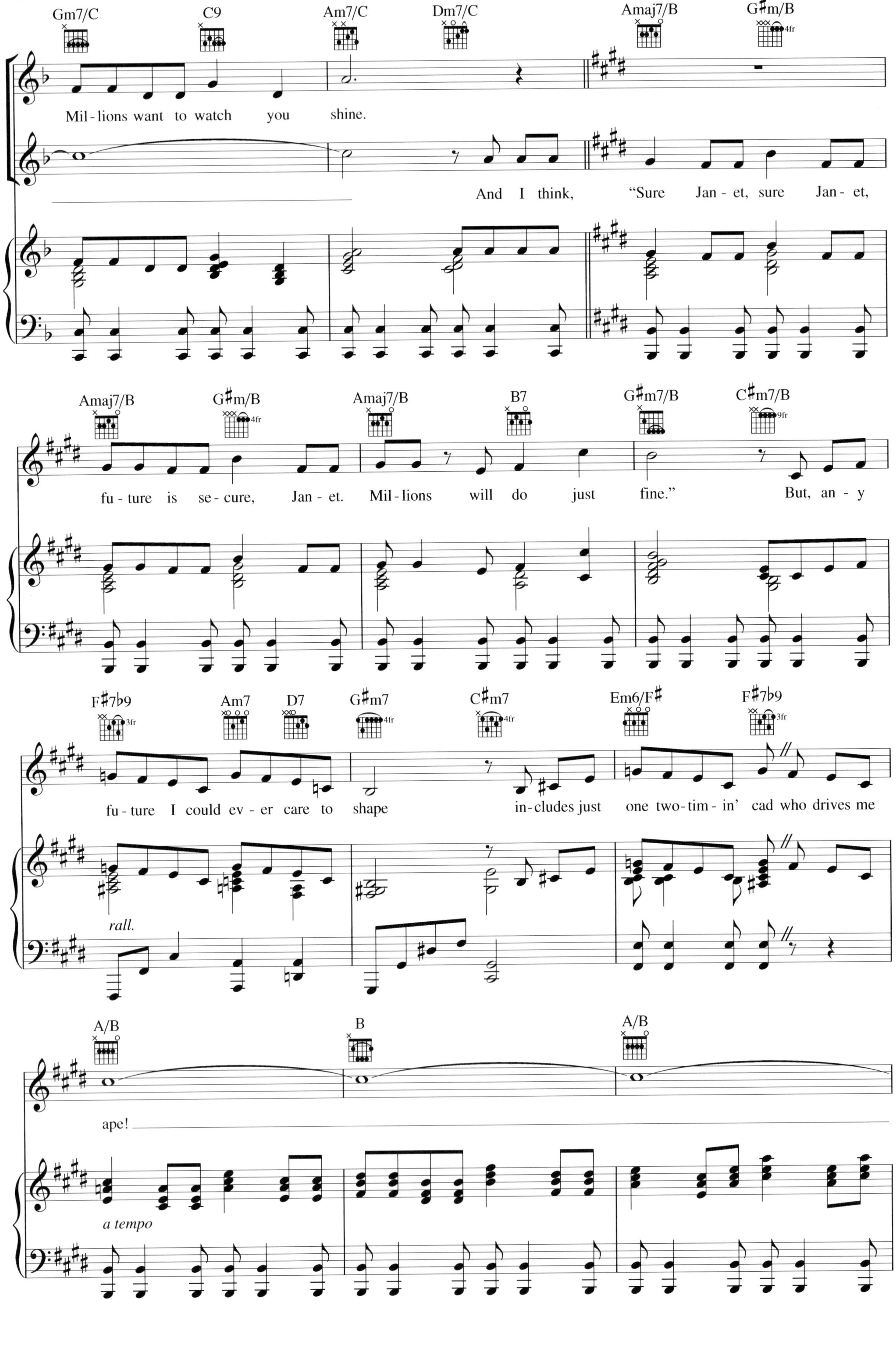

Gm7/C C9 Am7/C Dm7/C Amaj7/B G♯m/B
Mil - lions want to watch you shine.
And I think, "Sure Jan - et, sure Jan - et,
Amaj7/B G♯m/B Amaj7/B B7 G♯m7/B C♯m7/B
fu - ture is se - cure, Jan - et. Mil - lions will do just fine."
But, an - y
F♯7♭9 Am7 D7 G♯m7 C♯m7 Em6/F♯ F♯7♭9
fu - ture I could ev - er care to shape
in - cludes just one two - tim - in' cad who drives me
rall.
A/B B A/B
ape!
a tempo

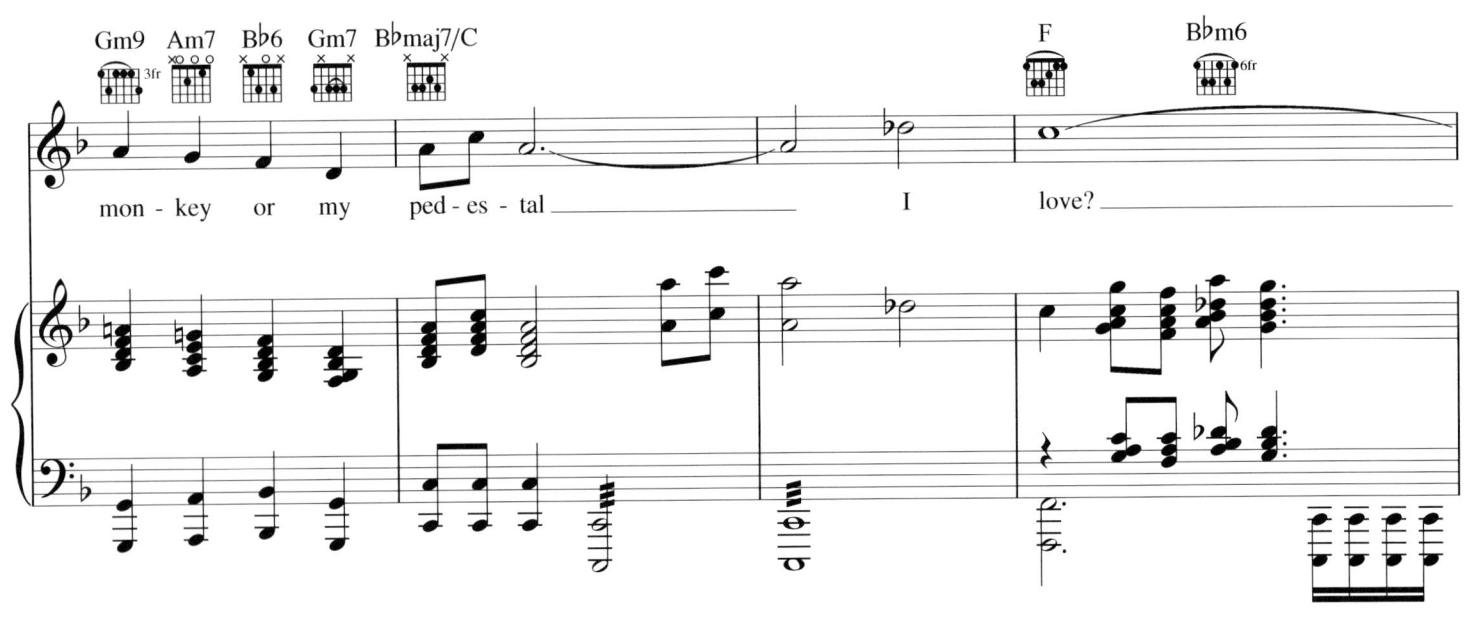
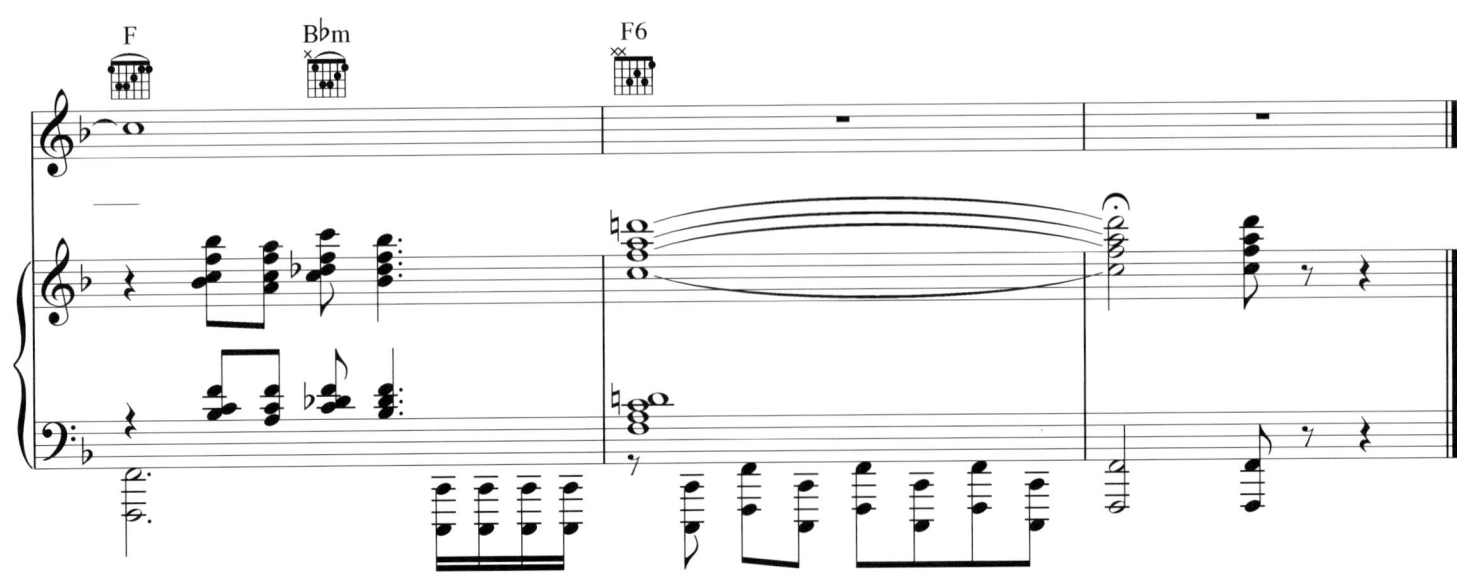

I DO, I DO IN THE SKY

Words and Music by LISA LAMBERT
and GREG MORRISON

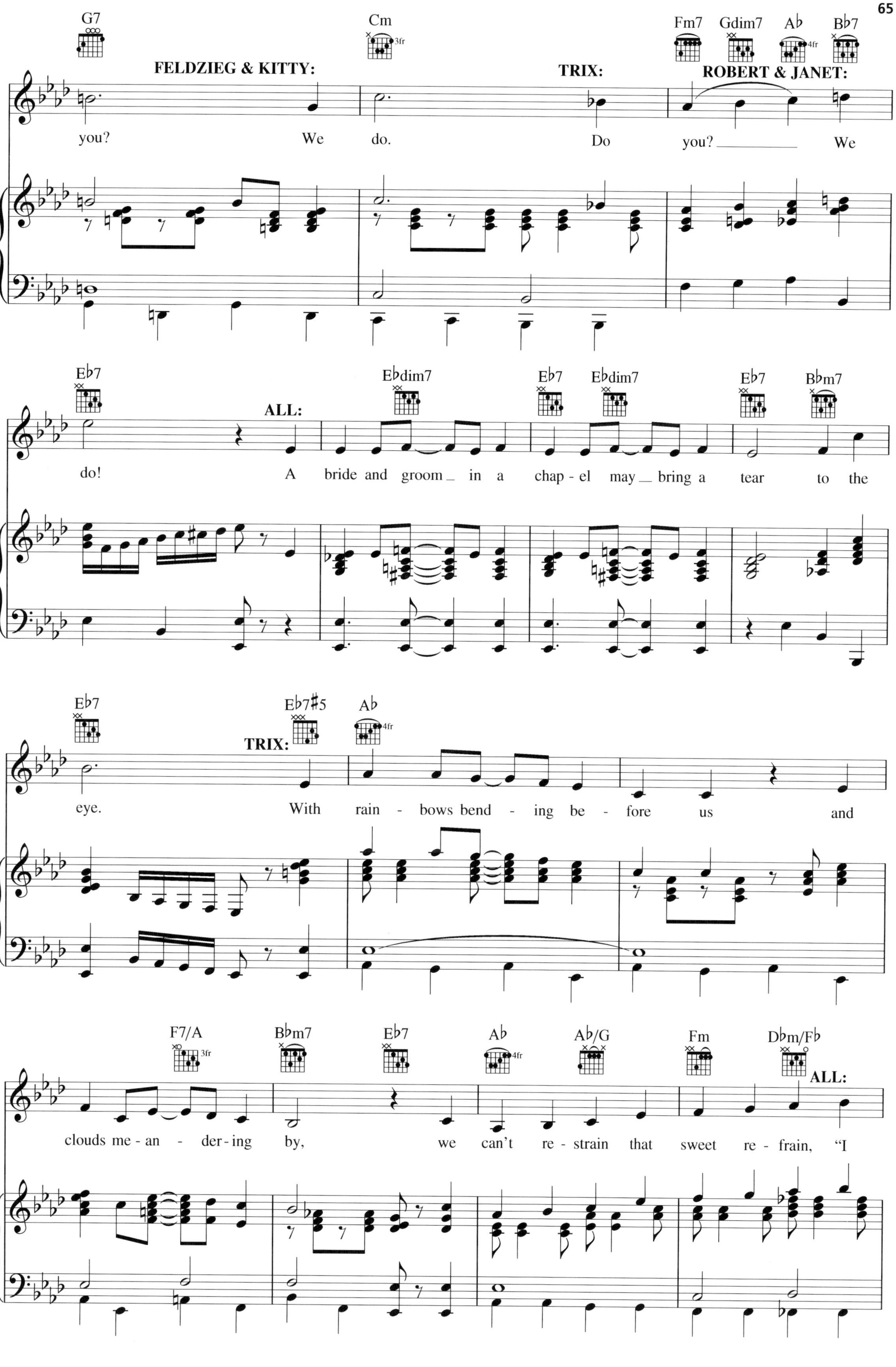
G7 Cm Fm7 Gdim7 A♭ B♭7
FEDZIEG & KITTY:
TRIX:
ROBERT & JANET:
you? We do. Do you? We
E♭7 E♭dim7 E♭7 E♭dim7 E♭7 B♭m7
ALL:
do! A bride and groom in a chap-el may bring a tear to the
E♭7 E♭7♯5 A♭
TRIX:
eye. With rain-bows bend-ing be-fore us and
F7/A B♭m7 E♭7 A♭ A♭/G Fm D♭m/F♭
ALL:
clouds me-an-der-ing by, we can't re-strain that sweet re-frain, "I

I REMEMBER LOVE

Words and Music by LISA LAMBERT and GREG MORRISON

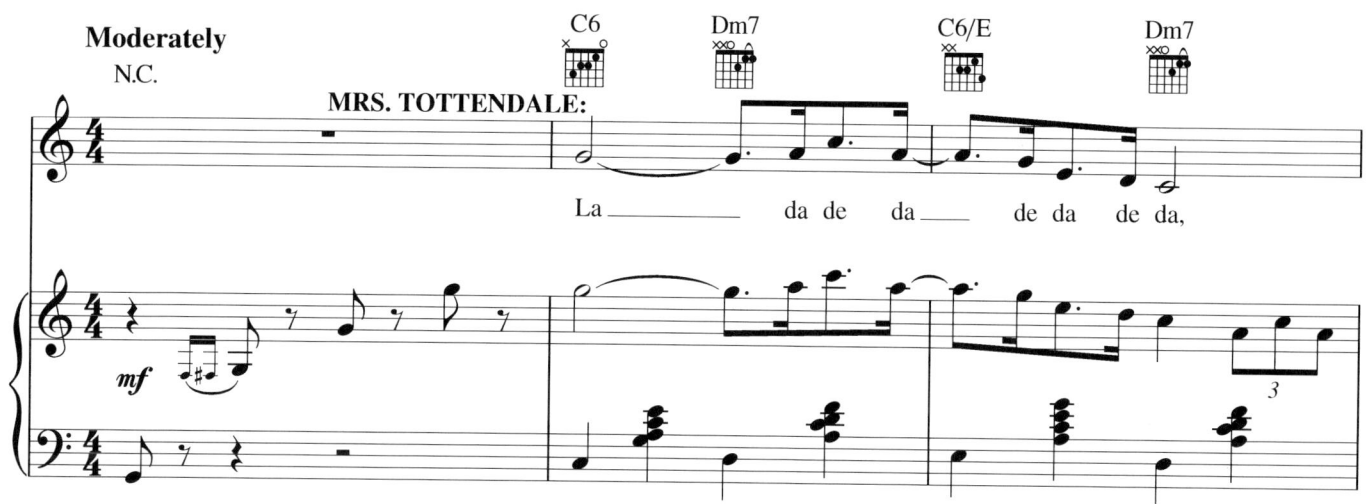

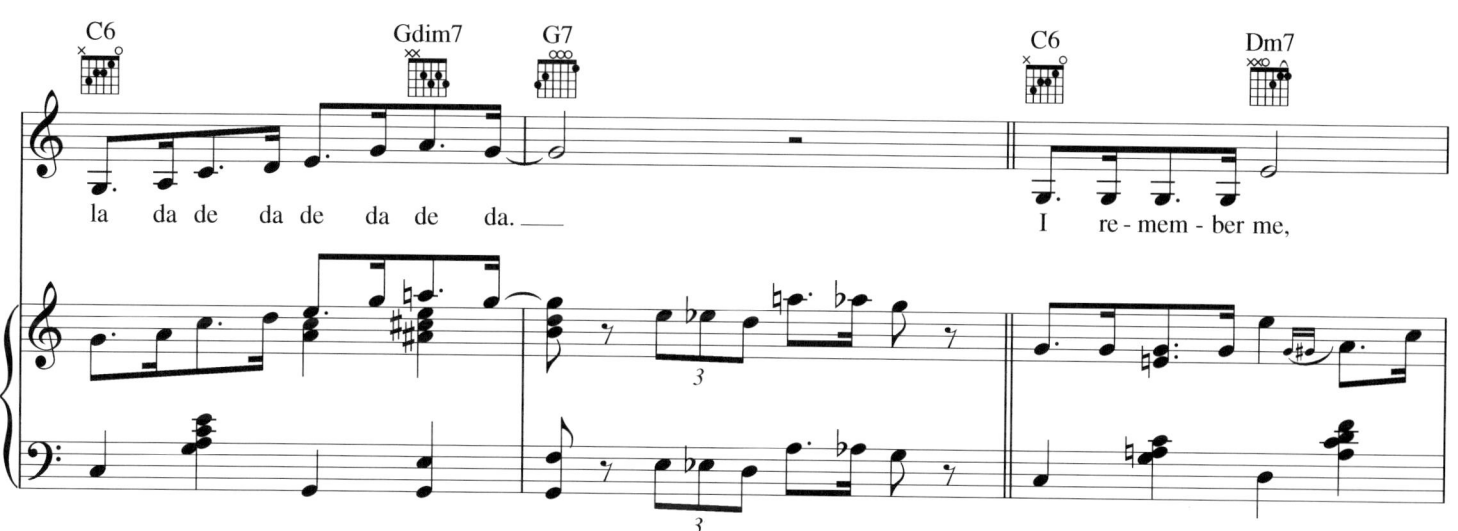

Copyright © 1999 Lisa Lambert and Gmorr Inc.
All Rights Reserved   Used by Permission

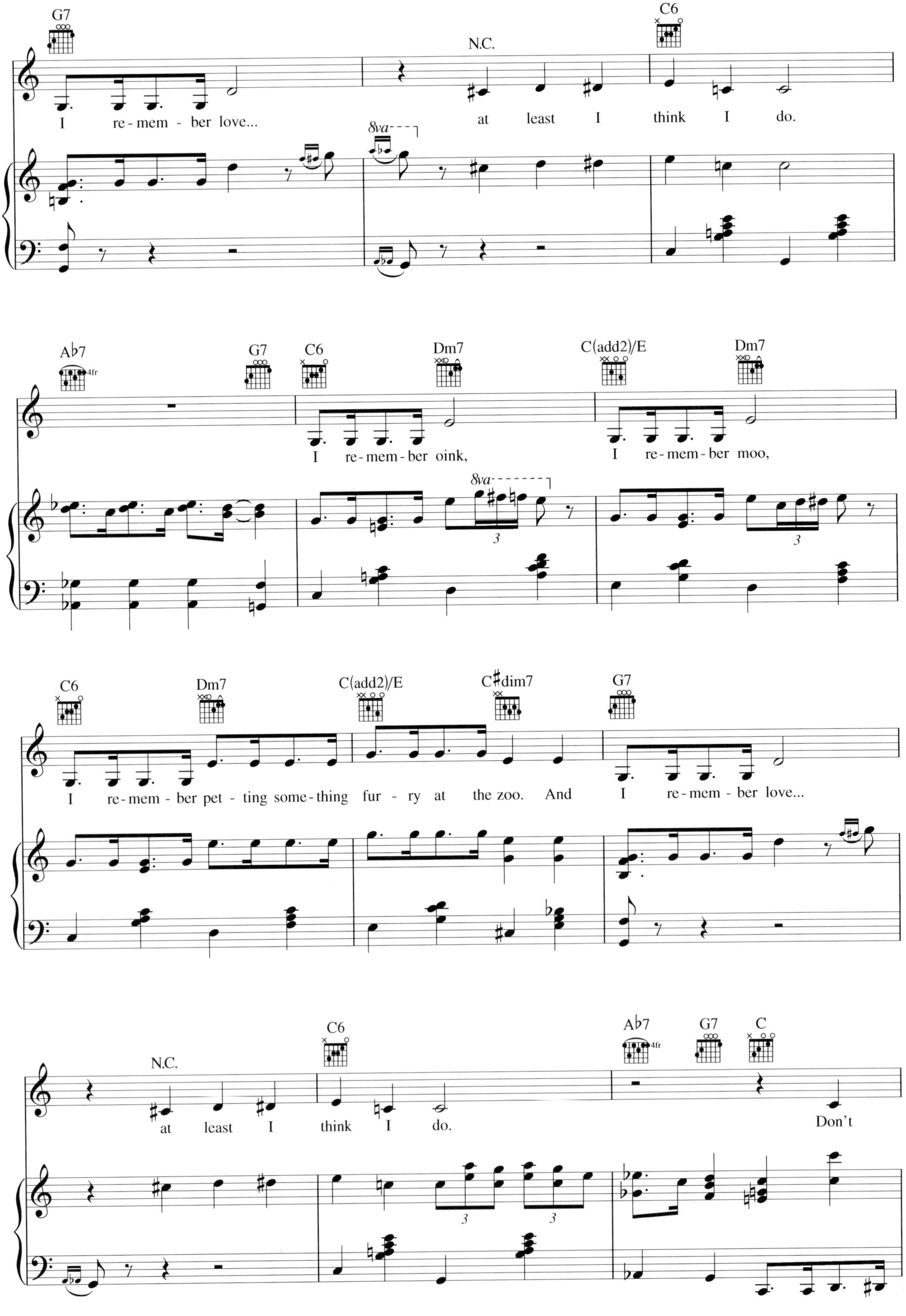
G7
N.C.
C6
I re-mem - ber love... at least I think I do.
8va
Ab7
G7
C6
Dm7
C(add2)/E
Dm7
I re-mem-ber oink, I re-mem-ber moo,
8va
C6
Dm7
C(add2)/E
C#dim7
G7
I re-mem - ber pet - ting some-thing fur - ry at the zoo. And I re-mem - ber love...
N.C.
C6
Ab7
G7
C
at least I think I do. Don't

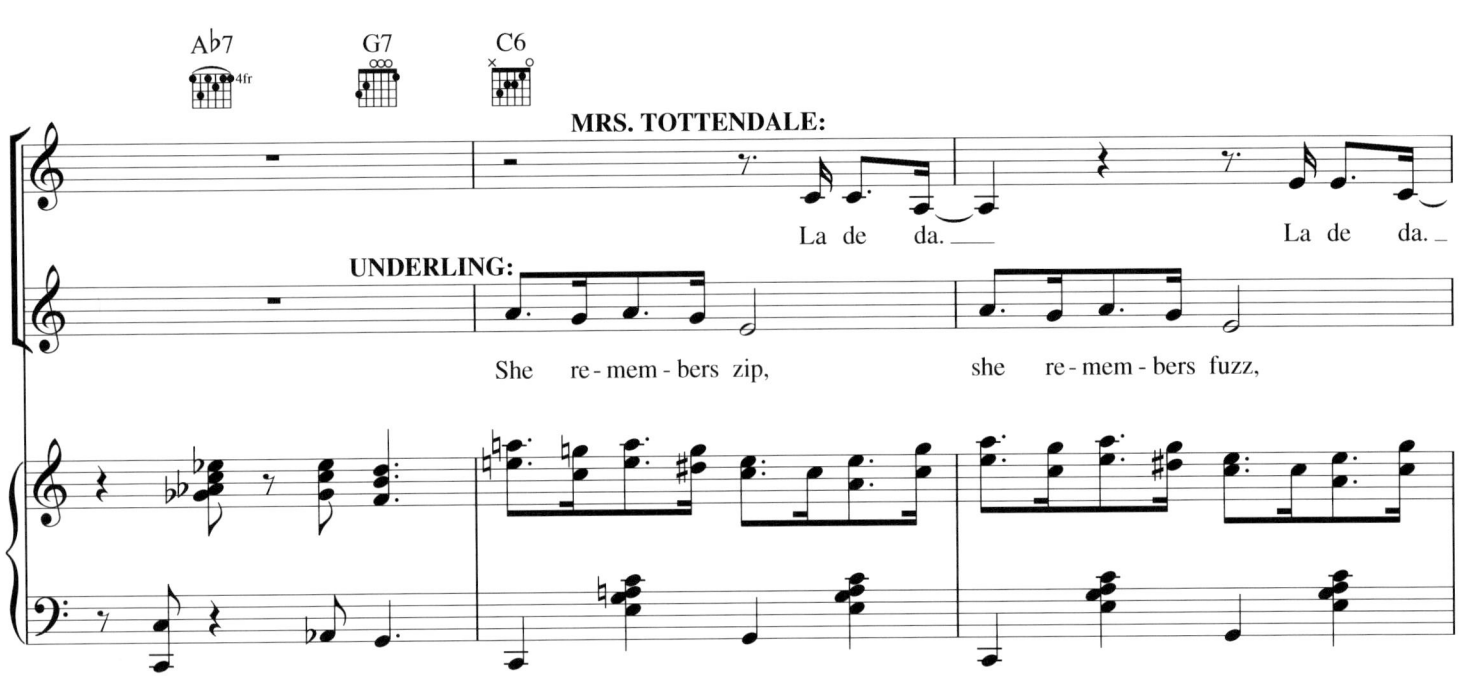

74